SKYJACK!

When people use guns to take what they want, how do you stop them? If you give them what they want, they will be happy – and they will use their guns again, and again. If you don't give them what they want, then they will be angry – and they will kill. It is not easy to decide what to do.

In this story, the person who has to decide is the Prime Minister, the head of the government. But the Prime Minister is also an ordinary person, just like the rest of us – a person with a family and children.

How can you think clearly, if someone is pointing a gun at your family? What do you do? You take advice, you talk to the hijackers, you find out what they want, you keep everybody calm, you try to move slowly. But terrorists don't like waiting, and sooner or later, you have to decide what to do . . .

OXFORD BOOKWORMS LIBRARY
Thriller & Adventure

Skyjack!

Stage 3 (1000 headwords)

Series Editor: Jennifer Bassett
Founder Editor: Tricia Hedge
Activities Editors: Jennifer Bassett and Alison Baxter

TIM VICARY

Skyjack!

OXFORD UNIVERSITY PRESS

Oxford University Press
Great Clarendon Street, Oxford OX2 6DP

Oxford   New York
Auckland Bangkok Buenos Aires Cape Town Chennai
Dar es Salaam Delhi Hong Kong Istanbul Karachi Kolkata
Kuala Lumpur Madrid Melbourne Mexico City Mumbai Nairobi
São Paulo Shanghai Taipei Tokyo Toronto

OXFORD and OXFORD ENGLISH
are trade marks of Oxford University Press

ISBN 0 19 423015 5

© Oxford University Press 2000
Ninth impression 2004

First published in Oxford Bookworms 1989
This second edition published in the Oxford Bookworms Library 2000

A complete recording of this Bookworms edition of *Skyjack!*
is available on cassette ISBN 0 19 422698 0

Illustrated by Ramsay Gibb

Printed in Spain by Unigraf s.l.

CONTENTS

1

The air hostess smiled. 'Welcome aboard, sir. Would you like a newspaper?'

'Yes, please.' Carl took the newspaper and looked at his ticket. 'I'm in seat 5F. Where's that?'

'It's near the front of the plane, sir. On the left, there. By the window.'

'I see. Thank you very much.' Carl smiled back at the air hostess. She was young and pretty. Just like my daughter, he thought.

He put his bag under his seat and sat down. His friend Harald sat beside him. They watched the other passengers coming onto the plane. Harald looked at his watch.

'9.30 p.m.,' he said. 'Good. We're on time.'

Carl agreed. 'And in three hours we'll be home,' he said. 'That's good. We've been away for a long time. You'll be pleased to see your family, won't you, Harald?'

Harald smiled. 'Yes, I will. Have you seen this, sir?' He opened his bag and took out two small planes. 'These are for my sons. I always bring something back for them.'

'How old are your sons?' Carl asked.

'Five and almost seven. The older one has a birthday tomorrow.'

'He'll be very excited tonight then.'

'Yes. I hope he gets some sleep.'

1

'Welcome aboard, sir.'

The plane took off. Carl watched the lights of the airport grow smaller below them. Then the plane flew above the clouds and he could see the moon and the stars in the night sky. He lay back in his seat and closed his eyes.

2

Later, he woke up. Harald was asleep. Carl looked at his watch. It was midnight. He called the air hostess.

'Excuse me. What time do we arrive?'

'11.30 p.m. local time, sir. That's about half an hour from now.'

'Thank you.' Carl changed the time on his watch.

'Anything else, sir?'

'No, I don't think so. Oh, wait a minute – could I have a cup of coffee, please?'

'Yes, of course, sir.' He watched her bring the coffee. 'She walks like my daughter, too,' he thought. 'And she is *very* young. She looks nervous, not sure what to do.'

'How long have you been an air hostess?' he asked.

She smiled. 'Three months, sir,' she said.

'Do you like it?'

'Yes, I love it. It's very exciting.' She smiled nervously. 'Will that be all, sir?'

'Yes, thank you.'

'Have a nice flight.'

He drank the coffee and started to read his newspaper. When Harald woke up, Carl showed him a page in the paper.

'Look. There you are,' he said. He pointed to a picture. In the middle of the picture stood Carl himself – a short thin man with grey hair, wearing a suit. Behind him, on the left, was Harald – a tall, strong young man, like a sportsman. Both men were smiling. 'That's you and me, outside the Embassy,' said Carl. 'We're in the news again. You can show it to your sons. You're a famous man, Harald!'

Harald laughed. 'You're the famous man, sir, not me,'

'I'm just a police officer.'

4

he said. 'I'm just a police officer. It's my job to take care of you. That's a photo of you, not me.'

'Perhaps. But your children think that you're a famous man, I'm sure. Here, take it, and show it to them.'

'OK. Thanks.' Harald smiled, and put the newspaper in his coat pocket. 'I think I'll have a cup of coffee too.' He called for the air hostess, but she did not come. Harald looked surprised.

'What's the matter?' Carl asked.

'The air hostess,' Harald said. 'She's sitting down talking to those two men.'

Carl looked up and saw the young air hostess. She was sitting in a seat at the front of the plane with two young men. They looked worried and nervous. Suddenly, one of the young men picked up a bag and *walked into the pilot's cabin*! The other man and the air hostess followed him.

'That's strange,' said Carl. 'What are they doing?'

'I don't know. It's very strange,' said Harald. 'I don't like it at all.' He began to get out of his seat, but then stopped and sat down again.

For one or two minutes nothing happened. None of the other passengers moved or spoke. They had seen the young men too. It became very quiet in the plane.

A bell rang, and for a moment they could hear two voices arguing. Then the pilot spoke.

'Ladies and gentlemen, this is the Captain speaking. Please do not be afraid. There is a change of plan. We

5

The air hostess had a machine gun in her hand.

have to land at another airport before we finish our journey. There's no danger. We will land in fifteen minutes. Please stay in your seats and keep calm. Thank you.'

Then the air hostess came out of the cabin. She looked very different now because she had a machine gun in her hand. She stood at the front of the plane and watched the passengers carefully.

3

'Here we are, madam.' The big black car stopped and a police officer opened the back door.

'Thank you.' Helen Sandberg smiled at him as she got out. Another police officer opened the front door of her house.

Inside the house it was quiet. Her daughter was reading. She put the book down.

'Hello, Mummy. You're late. You said you'd be home by ten o'clock. I wanted to talk to you about my homework, remember?'

Helen sat down. 'I'm sorry, Sarah. I did remember, really. But I had a very busy day. Anyway, I'm home now. What's the problem?'

'It's this book,' said Sarah. 'I have to write about it at school on Friday, and I don't understand it.'

'All right,' said Helen. 'Bring the book into the kitchen

and I'll look at it while you make me a cup of coffee.'

They sat in the kitchen and talked for nearly half an hour. Then Helen looked at her watch. 'OK, Sarah, that's enough for now. It's nearly midnight, and I must be up at six tomorrow. I'm going to bed. Goodnight.'

Alone in her bedroom, she undressed and got into the big empty bed. She was very tired. She closed her eyes and in three minutes she was asleep.

The phone rang at 12.15 a.m.

Helen groaned, and picked it up.

'Hello . . . What? . . . Who? . . . Do you know what time it is?'

She ran her hand through her hair and turned the light on. 'What, *now*? I don't believe it. Are you sure?'

The voice on the telephone explained carefully. Helen groaned again, and sat up. 'I hope it *is* serious. If it isn't, somebody is going to be in big trouble . . . yes . . . All right . . . Send the car in fifteen minutes, then. And bring me some coffee! Goodbye.'

She put the phone down and got out of bed. Outside the window she could hear a strong wind blowing.

Twenty minutes later she was sitting in the back of her big black car, drinking a cup of coffee and talking to the Chief of Airport Police on the car telephone. It was raining heavily.

Helen was talking to the Airport Police on the telephone.

Carl looked out of the plane window. It was very dark and rainy. It was a small airport with only one or two other planes. But there were three police cars near the airport building.

'I don't understand,' he said quietly in Harald's ear. 'Why are we here?'

Harald looked worried. 'Don't ask me,' he whispered back. 'Ask them.'

'No thanks.' Carl looked at the hijackers. The young air hostess was still standing at the front of the plane with her machine gun. One of the young men, also with a machine gun, was standing at the back of the plane. The other hijacker was in the Captain's cabin. All the passengers sat very quietly in their seats.

A bell rang and a man's voice spoke.

'Ladies and gentlemen, listen to me. This is the People's Liberation Army. This plane is ours now, and you are our prisoners. We do not want to hurt you, but as you can see, we have our guns and we know how to shoot. So please, sit quietly in your seats and do what we say. We will be here for one or two hours. The Government of this country has two of our brothers in a prison near this airport. We are asking the Government to bring our two brothers to this plane. When our

brothers are free, you will be free. We think this will take one or two hours, but not very long. As you know, the Prime Minister of this country is only a woman. She will do what we say. So do not worry. Just sit very still and wait a little while. Goodnight.'

Carl looked at Harald. 'Oh dear,' he whispered. 'I think we're in trouble, my young friend. Big trouble.'

Harald agreed. 'We certainly are. The Government won't set those two men free. They tried to put a bomb on a plane last year, didn't they, sir? They're in prison for thirty years!'

'I know,' Carl whispered. 'No one could set them free. So what about us?'

'What about *you*, you mean,' whispered Harald. 'I'm not important. Look, sir, you'd better give me your passport.'

'What? Why?'

'Ssh!' Harald put his hand on the older man's arm and stopped talking. Carl looked up and saw the young air hostess staring at them. Her machine gun was pointing at them too. He stopped talking and looked out of the window.

After a few minutes she stopped watching them. 'Give me the passport, sir!' Harald whispered, very quietly. Very slowly and carefully, Carl took it out of his pocket and gave it to him.

There was still some coffee in Carl's cup. Very carefully, Harald put the passport on his tray and poured

11

Harald tore the passport into pieces. Then he ate them!

the coffee onto it. When the passport was very wet, he
tore it slowly into little pieces. He was a strong young
man and because the passport was wet, it did not make a
sound. Then, one by one, he put the pieces of wet paper
into his mouth and ate them. In ten minutes, the passport
had disappeared.

'I don't understand,' whispered Carl. 'Why did you do
that?'

'You'll see,' whispered Harald. 'But when they ask
questions, let me answer, sir. OK? You say nothing.'

'OK.' Carl looked away, out of the window. A large
black car was just driving up to the airport building.

5

The black car stopped outside the airport building
and a police officer opened the door. Helen Sandberg
got out and went quickly inside. Upstairs, in the control
room, the Chief of Airport Police, Inspector Holm, was
waiting with a soldier. Helen's secretary, Michael, was
there too.

'Good evening, Prime Minister,' said Inspector Holm.
'This is Colonel Carter, of the Special Commando
Section.'

'Good evening, Colonel.' Helen shook hands with the
soldier and looked at him. He was a thin, tough-looking
man, about forty years old, with a brown face. His hand

13

was hard and strong. 'I hope you know your job,' she thought. 'I may need you.'

She looked out of the window. There was a large plane on the tarmac about two hundred metres away. All its lights were on. 'Is that the plane?' she asked.

'That's it, Prime Minister.'

'Right, give me the facts. How many people are on it?'

Inspector Holm answered. 'One hundred and eight passengers, five crew.'

'What nationalities are they?'

'There are twenty-nine Americans, fifteen British, two Brazilians, two Indians, and one Chinese. The others are from this country.'

'I see. There are a lot of Americans and British, then,' said Helen quietly. 'That means trouble.'

'Yes, Prime Minister,' answered Michael. 'I'm afraid their Ambassadors are on their way here now.'

Helen smiled at him quickly. He was a good secretary; he usually knew what she was thinking. Both the American Ambassador and the British Ambassador were difficult people.

She turned back to Inspector Holm. 'Tell me about the hijackers. What do they want?'

'We don't know how many hijackers there are, Prime Minister. But they have guns, we know that. They say they are from the People's Liberation Army. And they want three things.' Inspector Holm paused and looked down at her. He was a very tall man and he looked very important in his uniform. Helen didn't like him much.

'Yes, well. What three things?' she asked quickly.

'Firstly, they say we must set free their two brothers from prison. You remember, Prime Minister – two men tried to put a bomb on a plane last year. They are in prison near here.'

'I remember,' Helen answered softly. 'They're in prison for thirty years, aren't they?'

'I think so. Something like that.' The man paused. 'Secondly, they say we must refuel the plane because they want to fly to another country. Thirdly, they say we must put this in all our newspapers. It says they are fighting for freedom for their people. They are freedom fighters. They want to liberate their people.'

He gave her a sheet of paper. Helen put it on the table. She did not read it. 'And what about the passengers?' she asked. 'When will the hijackers set them free?'

'They say they will set most of the passengers free when their brothers are on the plane. But they want ten passengers to fly away with them. They will set them free when they arrive.'

'I see.'

'There's one other thing, Prime Minister,' Colonel Carter spoke for the first time. His voice was very quiet, almost gentle. 'They say we must bring the prisoners to the airport in two hours. If not, they will kill a passenger. They said this one hour ago.'

'So we have one hour left?'

15

'That's right, Prime Minister. Just one hour. Then they will kill the first passenger.'

'I see.' Helen walked slowly to the window and stared out at the plane. It was still raining and a strong wind was blowing. She turned round. 'Thank you, gentlemen. I will have to talk to them. But first I need a few minutes to think. Colonel Carter, Inspector, please go to the other room. Tell the hijackers I will talk to them in five minutes. Michael, stay here.'

'But . . . yes, madam.' Inspector Holm looked unhappy, but he went out, slowly, with the Colonel. Michael sat quietly, looking at her. He knew what she was thinking.

'Have you got the passenger list, Michael?'

'Yes, Prime Minister. Here you are.'

She picked up the list of names and looked at it carefully. 'Oh my God!' His name was near the beginning. She dropped the list, sat down at the table, and ran her hands through her hair. For a long minute she said nothing. Then she looked up.

'This is going to be very difficult, isn't it, Michael?'

'I'm afraid so, Prime Minister. Very difficult indeed.'

Helen stood up and walked to the window, thinking hard. Outside in the rain, the American Ambassador's car stopped by the door.

'Just one hour. Then they'll kill the first passenger.'

6

Carl looked through the window and watched the cars arrive at the airport building. There were a lot of cars now and a lot of lights in the building. Inside the plane it was hot and quiet. There was nothing to do. He remembered other times when he had been in a plane at night with his wife and daughter. That had been fun because they were excited and going on holiday. His daughter had always asked lots of questions in the plane. Now no one said anything at all. Carl sat, and thought, and felt his face becoming wet with sweat.

'Your passports, please!'

'What?' He turned suddenly. One of the hijackers, a young man in a black shirt, was just behind them. He had a bag in his hand and he was taking everyone's passports and putting them in it.

'Why . . . ?'

'Be quiet!' Harald whispered. 'Let me talk, sir. Remember?'

'Your passports, please.' The young man stood by their seats.

'Here you are.' Harald gave the man his passport.

'Thank you. And his?'

'He has no passport. I am a police officer and he is my prisoner. I am taking him to prison in my country.'

'I see.' The young man looked at them both in surprise. 'Stand up, you!'

Carl stood up and the young man searched his pockets, but he found nothing. He told Carl to sit down, then he opened Harald's passport and looked inside. 'Police pig!' he said. 'Now you are our prisoner!' Then he hit Harald in the face, looked at Carl, and laughed. 'And perhaps we will set him free!'

Harald said nothing. The hijacker was about the same age as him, but not so big. The young hijacker laughed again and moved on to the next seat.

'Thank you, Harald,' Carl whispered, when the man was at the front of the plane. 'That was very brave. But I won't let you die for me, you know.'

'Be quiet, sir! Something's happening!' Harald whispered back.

Carl looked up. Another hijacker was standing in the door of the Captain's cabin. He was talking to the other two. He was a big strong man, with a black beard. He looked angry and waved his arms. Carl listened carefully. He could hear one or two words, but not many.

'. . . nothing! Nothing at all! . . . stupid woman! . . . she needs time, she says . . .'

All the hijackers were angry now. They looked at the passports and then started to walk down the aisle, pointing their guns at the passengers. Harald sat very still in his seat.

19

'Don't look at them, Carl,' he whispered. 'Sit very still and don't look at them.'

Suddenly the big hijacker pulled a passenger out of his seat. The passenger was a short fat man in a grey suit. He shouted angrily in a voice that sounded American, but the hijacker hit him and then pushed him to the front of the plane with his machine gun.

'Turn towards the door!' he shouted. 'Put your hands on the door! Above your head! Higher! That's it!'

The air hostess pointed her gun at the American's back. The hijacker in the black shirt stood at the front of the plane and pointed his gun at the passengers.

'Don't move!' he shouted. 'Stay in your seats and don't look back!' Then the big bearded hijacker went back into the Captain's cabin.

The bell rang. The hijacker's voice spoke.

'Passengers! Listen to me! You know we are here to set our brothers free. I have spoken to the Prime Minister of this country. I told her she must bring our brothers here by two o'clock. That is plenty of time because the prison is only ten kilometres from here. She says she needs more time, but we know she is lying. We have no time. The passenger at the front of the plane is an American spy who lives in our country. All Americans who live in our country are spies. If our brothers are not here at two o'clock, he will die. If you try to help him, you will die too.'

'Jesus,' Carl said quietly. He looked at his watch. The time was 1.50 a.m. He looked out of the window across

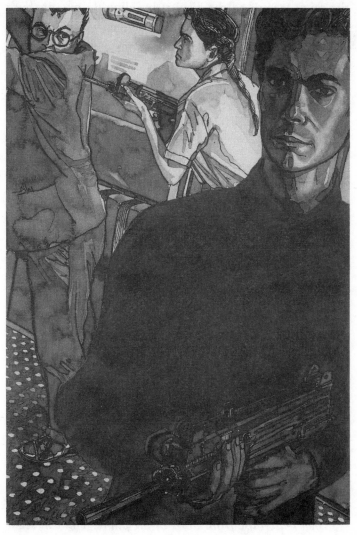

The air hostess pointed her gun at the American's back.

the rainy tarmac to the airport building. In one of those rooms was the Prime Minister. What would she do? What *could* she do? 'Come on, honey,' he said softly. 'Start thinking. Think fast, honey. And think hard!'

7

Helen Sandberg sat at the radio in the control room. Michael, Inspector Holm, and Colonel Carter sat behind her. They could all see the plane, two hundred metres away, and they could all hear the voice of the hijacker on the radio. It was loud, excited.

'*Our brothers have done nothing wrong. They are innocent! They are fighters for the freedom of our people! We need them with us on this plane, now!*'

Helen kept her voice low and calm. 'Look, I understand what you say. But those men are criminals; they're in prison. I can't bring them here. And remember, the passengers on the plane are innocent people too, with families and children. Please set them free. We will not hurt you. We . . .'

The voice on the radio interrupted her. '*Mrs Sandberg! I do not want to talk any more. It is now 1.59 a.m. Do you have our brothers here, at the airport?*'

'No. I told you . . .'

'*Then watch the front door of the plane. You can see it well, I hope?*'

'Yes.' Helen's voice was quiet now, almost a whisper.

'Then watch. There is an American spy behind it. And remember, we have many American spies, and many important business people on this plane. In half an hour I will ask you again about my brothers.'

Helen stared out at the plane. Its front door was very small and far away. Colonel Carter touched her arm.

'Here are some binoculars, Prime Minister. You will be able to see more clearly with these.'

She did not want to look, but she had to. She had decided not to free the prisoners, so now she had to see what happened to the passengers. She picked up the binoculars and stared at the front door of the plane.

The door opened slowly. There were no steps outside the door, so it was about four metres above the ground. Standing in the door was a short fat man, his hands above his head. His face was white and he looked very frightened. Then he jumped. But as he jumped, a girl came to the door and shot him. Some bullets hit him in the air and more bullets hit him as he lay on the ground. One of his arms moved a little and blood ran out of the side of his head onto the wet tarmac. The girl continued shooting him for ten, maybe fifteen seconds. Then someone pulled her back into the plane and the door closed.

For a long time everyone was silent. Then Colonel Carter spoke. 'Inspector, why didn't your men shoot? That girl was in the doorway for nearly fifteen seconds! Why isn't she dead?'

23

'We . . . are police officers, not soldiers. I . . .' But the Colonel interrupted him.

'Prime Minister, let my men deal with this problem. They have killed a man now and they'll kill another one in half an hour. We must attack that plane! We are commandos; we know how to do it!'

Helen was still watching the dead body of the man on the tarmac. She thought a hand moved, for a moment; but no, he must be dead by now. There was a pool of blood on the tarmac now, around his head. He could not possibly be alive. For a moment she did not hear the voices around her. In half an hour . . .

'Prime Minister . . . ?'

'Yes.' She turned towards them. 'Yes. Colonel Carter, bring your men here, immediately. Meet me in ten minutes with your plan. But I warn you, it must be a good one. I don't want any more dead passengers.'

'Yes, Prime Minister. At once.' The Colonel turned to go.

'Inspector.'

'Yes, madam.'

'I want those two prisoners brought here from the prison. At once. You have twenty-five minutes, no more. Do you understand?'

'But Prime Minister! You can't do that!' The Inspector and the Colonel stared at her in surprise.

'I can and I will.'

'But these men are dangerous criminals – terrorists!

24

There was a pool of blood on the tarmac, around his head.

They tried to put a bomb on a plane! They are in prison for . . .'

'For thirty years, Colonel. I know. But they are only two men, and there are over a hundred innocent people on that plane. My job is to save their lives, and I need time to do it.'

The Inspector stood up very tall and straight in his fine uniform. 'Prime Minister, I strongly advise you not to do this. You don't understand . . .'

Helen interrupted him, her voice ice-cold and angry. 'I understand very well indeed, Inspector. And I thank you for your advice. But I think I must make the decisions, and you must obey my orders. You now have only twenty-four minutes. Bring those prisoners here, please.'

'Yes, madam.' The Inspector and the Colonel left the room, looking very unhappy.

'Prime Minister?'

'Yes, Michael?' She turned, and saw that Michael was smiling quietly.

'The American and British Ambassadors are here. Do you want to see them?'

She groaned, and sat down suddenly. 'Do I want to? Of course I don't! But I suppose I must talk to them because that man was an American. Send them in. They can have five minutes with me, that's all.'

'Yes, Prime Minister.' Michael picked up a telephone.

8

When the girl came back into the cabin she was shaking. Her hands were shaking and she was crying and smoke was coming out of her gun. One of the passengers, an American, stood up and shouted at her.

'You're a murderer!' he shouted. 'You're a dirty, murdering b . . .'

She turned and pointed the gun at him and fired. The man sat down in his seat and the bullets went above the seats, all along the plane, and out through the roof. After ten seconds the girl stopped firing and shouted.

'You shut up! You shut up and sit down or I'll kill you all! I am a soldier of the People's Liberation Army and I'll kill you, all of you!' But she was crying too, and the young man in the black shirt put his arm around her and held her. She leaned against him, crying, and he whispered something in her ear.

It was then that Harald moved. He got out of his seat, bent low, and ran very fast along the aisle towards the front of the plane. The young man and the girl did not see him coming and he caught them both around their legs and knocked them onto the floor. Harald fell on top of them and he tried to take one of the guns, but the girl pulled his hair and the young man held his arms. Then the bearded man came out of the Captain's cabin and hit

Harald ran very fast along the aisle.

Harald hard on the head with his gun. Harald fell on the floor and lay still. The bearded man pointed his gun at the passengers and shouted 'SIT STILL!' very loud indeed.

None of the passengers had moved except Carl, and he was too slow. He stood very still in the middle of the aisle five metres away from the bearded man's gun. The other two hijackers were still on the floor, and Carl saw the Captain move in the cabin behind the bearded man. But the young man in the black shirt saw him too, and stood up and pointed his gun at the Captain. Both Carl and the Captain were too late.

'I am getting old,' Carl thought. 'When I was young, I could move as fast as Harald. But not now.' Carl sat down in his seat, very slowly. The bearded man watched him all the time. He pushed Harald with his foot.

'Search him,' he said to the girl. 'Then handcuff him to the door. He will be the next one.'

The girl pulled Harald to the door. She found some handcuffs in his pocket and handcuffed him to the door. Then she searched his other pockets.

In one of his pockets she found a newspaper. She looked at it and saw the photo of Harald and Carl. She stood up slowly and showed it to the bearded man. He looked at the photo, and then he looked at Carl carefully and for a long time. Very slowly smiles appeared on the faces of the two hijackers and they began to laugh.

The hijacker looked at the photo, and then at Carl.

9

Helen Sandberg stood up to welcome the American and British Ambassadors. The two men were very different. The American Ambassador was a short round man with a loud voice which Helen disliked very much. He often wore open-necked shirts, and he had a very hairy chest. She disliked that too. The British Ambassador – a tall thin Scotsman from Edinburgh – was always quiet, polite and well-dressed, but she did not always believe what he said. Once – a year ago – he had lied to her and she could never forget that.

But most of all, she disliked them because they were

both military men and their countries were much bigger than hers. They wanted military bases for their soldiers in her country and she did not want them.

'So, gentlemen, what can I do for you?'

The American spoke first. 'Well, ma'am, an American passenger is dead . . . .'

'Yes, I know. I am very sorry about that. I hope no more will die.'

'I hope so too, ma'am. There are twenty-eight US passengers on that plane and my Government wants to keep them alive.'

'There are a hundred and seven passengers on that plane, Ambassador, and my Government wants them all alive,' Helen answered quietly. But the Ambassador did not listen.

'So the US Government is going to help you, ma'am. We have fifty US Marines at the US Embassy, and they can be here in one hour from now. Then they'll just take that goddam plane apart.'

The Scotsman smiled. 'Excuse me, Ambassador, but perhaps one hour from now will be too late. One man is already dead. But, er . . . perhaps you don't know this, Prime Minister, but this week six SAS soldiers are visiting the British Embassy, and they're waiting outside in my car now. These men know a lot about hijacks; much more than the US Marines or, probably, your own soldiers, Prime Minister. They know exactly what to do. So . . .'

31

'Now just a moment!' The American interrupted. 'The US Marines are . . .'

'*Gentlemen!*' Helen's clear, hard voice stopped them. 'There's no time to argue. Firstly, I didn't know about the SAS soldiers in the British Embassy, and I am very surprised about it. Very surprised indeed, Ambassador. Secondly, I do not think it is a good idea to attack a plane with a hundred and seven passengers in it, and "take it apart" as you say. I want these people to live, not die. So I thank you for your ideas, but remember that this small country is ours, not yours. We will manage this problem in our own way, with our own people, thank you very much. Now you must excuse me, I am busy.'

At the door, the Scotsman turned back. 'Prime Minister, I know you want to save lives,' he said. 'I understand that. But these hijackers must not go free. My Government does not want that. No Government in the world wants that.'

'I know that, Ambassador,' Helen answered quietly. 'I know that very well.'

As they went out, the phone rang. Michael picked it up. Helen sat down at the table and watched him. His face was very serious. He wrote on a piece of paper and then put the phone down. For a moment, he did not look at her.

'What is it, Michael? Tell me.'

'It was a radio message from the plane, Prime Minister.'

'Well? What did they say? Didn't they want to talk to me?'

'No, Prime Minister. Just the message. It says: "*We love our brothers. We hope the Prime Minister loves her husband. He is on the plane, just behind the door.*"'

For a long moment she stared at Michael, but she did not speak. A picture of the American passenger appeared in her head. She saw him jumping out of the door and the girl shooting him. Shooting him for ten, maybe fifteen long seconds.

'I'm sorry, Prime Minister,' said Michael softly.

'What? Yes, so am I. I thought perhaps . . . perhaps the hijackers didn't know Carl was my husband. But now they do know.'

She ran her hand through her hair and then looked at her watch. But her hand was shaking so much that she could not tell the time.

The phone rang again. Michael picked it up.

'Colonel Carter is outside, Prime Minister.' He watched her, waiting for an answer. 'I'll tell him to wait, shall I?'

She put her hands flat on the table and stood up. 'Yes. Yes, Michael. Tell him to wait two minutes, that's all.' She walked to the window and stared out at the plane. She pressed her forehead against the cool glass and for two minutes she did not move. Then she turned round and smiled at Michael.

'Let's just hope Colonel Carter's plan is a good one, shall we? Show him in.'

'We hope the Prime Minister loves her husband.'

10

In the plane, Carl and Harald sat on the floor by the door. They were handcuffed together with Harald's handcuffs. The girl hijacker stood watching them with her gun. The bearded man was in the Captain's cabin, and the young man in the black shirt was watching the other passengers.

Harald touched his head with his hand. There was blood in his hair.

'How do you feel, my young friend?' Carl asked.

'It hurts,' Harald answered. 'And I can't see well.'

'This man needs a doctor,' Carl said to the girl, angrily.

She laughed. 'That is your wife's problem, not mine,' she said. 'If our brothers come, he will get a doctor. If they don't come, he won't need one.' She pointed her gun at Harald's head and laughed again. She wasn't at all nervous now.

Carl felt angry. He was angry with the hijackers and he was angry with himself because he had not moved fast enough to help Harald. It was good to be angry; when he was angry he did not feel so afraid.

'How old are you?' he asked the girl.

She did not answer.

'I asked you a question!' he said. 'How old are you? Eighteen, nineteen? You're not very old, really, are you? You're just a child!'

The girl's face went red. 'I'm twenty,' she said angrily. 'I'm not a child!'

'You look like a child,' Carl said. 'You're only two years older than my daughter. Why are you doing this?'

The girl laughed. She didn't look at his eyes. 'Why? You wouldn't understand.'

'I don't think you understand what you're doing,' Carl said. 'None of the people in this plane has hurt you. We are all innocent. That man you killed – he wasn't a spy, he was just an American businessman. You've never seen any of us before. Why do you want to kill us?'

The girl looked worried and angry. She pointed the gun straight at Carl's head. 'I don't want to kill you,' she said. 'I want your government – your wife – to set our brothers free.'

'Yes, I know,' said Carl, carefully. He watched the gun and the girl's face, but he was not really afraid because he was still angry. He argued with the girl as though he was arguing with his daughter. 'But remember what your brothers did. They tried to put a bomb on a plane. They wanted to kill innocent people like us. Why?'

'You are not innocent!' said the girl. 'No one is innocent! People like you, and your wife, and that American – you have money and power and you take it from my people, from us! Do you know how I lived when I was a child? Ten people in one room, with no bath, no water, nothing! My parents had no jobs, no passports, no country, nothing! We lived in a town with ten thousand

36

'*I want your government to set our brothers free.*'

others. But ten kilometres away there were rich people like you, with big beautiful houses, fine cars, fine clothes – and they were all *innocent* people, like you! I tell you no one is innocent!'

She was shouting now, and nearly crying – there were tears in her eyes. Carl and Harald watched the gun carefully. 'Poor girl,' Carl thought. 'Poor little murderess.'

The bearded man came out of the Captain's cabin and put his hand on the girl's arm. 'Stop it, little flower,' he said. 'Don't talk to them. That's not your job.' Then he hit Carl in the face. 'Keep your mouth shut!' he said. 'Think about your wife instead. Do you see the time? I think she has forgotten you!'

Carl groaned and held his mouth with his hand. There was blood in his mouth and one of his teeth was broken. Then he looked at his watch. It was 2.23. Seven minutes left; then the half hour was over.

'I'm sorry, my friend,' he whispered to Harald. 'You tried fighting, and I tried talking. But it didn't work. I think this may be our last journey.'

11

Helen Sandberg decided she liked Colonel Carter. He spoke clearly, he explained his ideas carefully, and he listened to what she said. He did not try to be difficult because she was a woman. Best of all, they had made a plan together. A good plan, she thought; it could really work. Perhaps.

She looked at her watch: 2.23. 'Right, Colonel, get your men ready. I'll send the first prisoner down to you when they arrive. But where are they? Michael, have they arrived yet?'

'No, Prime Minister. Not yet.'

'Then where the hell are they? Can you get Inspector Holm on the car radio?'

'They're trying, Prime Minister.' Michael spoke into the telephone. Colonel Carter left the room and Helen walked up and down slowly, watching the clock. 2.24. 2.25. 2.26.

'They've got him, Prime Minister! He says . . . he says one of the cars has had an accident in the rain. He thinks he can be here in ten minutes.' Michael looked up. There was no smile on his face at all now.

'Ten minutes! What's he driving – a police car, or a bicycle?' Helen banged her fist on the table. 'We've got four minutes left. OK. I want to talk to the hijackers. Get them on the radio.'

She sat down at the table while Michael called the plane. Colonel Carter came in and stood behind her. A voice came on the radio.

'*Well, Mrs Sandberg. Where are our brothers?*'

'They're coming,' said Helen. 'They'll be here in ten minutes.'

'If my brothers are not here in four minutes, your husband will die.'

'*That is too late. I gave you half an hour. Your husband will die in four minutes.*'

Helen pressed her hands flat on the table, so hard that the ends of her fingers went white. 'Please don't do that,' she said.

'*I am sorry, Mrs Sandberg. But if my brothers are not here in four minutes, your husband will die.*'

'Don't you want to see your brothers?' she asked quickly. 'I promise you, if you kill my husband, you'll never see them again.'

There was a pause while no one spoke. Then the radio answered. '*Four minutes, Mrs Sandberg.*'

Helen spoke clearly, slowly, and loudly. She filled her voice with all the anger she had in her body. 'Listen, you murderer. I need just ten minutes to get your brothers to this airport. Then I will send them to the plane. But if you kill my husband, or anyone else, then I promise you that your brothers will die, on the tarmac in front of that plane. Is that what you want? Or will you wait ten minutes?'

There was another, longer pause. Helen stared out into the night. She did not see anything.

'*All right. Ten more minutes.*'

'Thank you. Now, there is one more thing. The passengers.'

'*What about them?*'

'You must set them free before I send your brothers to the plane.'

41

The voice on the radio laughed. '*Because you are a woman, do you think all men are stupid, like your husband? Send me our brothers, then refuel the plane, and then I will send you the passengers.*'

'No,' answered Helen. She looked at Colonel Carter. 'This is how we will do it. I will send you one of your brothers and then you must send me the passengers. When we have all the passengers, then we will refuel the plane and send you your other brother.'

The voice laughed again. '*Do you think you are buying cheap fish from a child in the market? Send us one brother, then, and we will send you one hundred passengers. Refuel the plane and send us the other brother, and we will send you the other passengers. But the pilot and your husband must come with us to another country. We will set them free later.*'

Helen looked at Colonel Carter. There was the beginning of a smile on her face. She could see that he agreed with her. She waited for a moment longer, to worry the hijacker.

'*Is it agreed, woman? Or do I kill your husband now?*'

'I agree. I will send your first brother to you in ten minutes.'

12

Carl felt his broken tooth with his tongue. The door of the Captain's cabin was open and he could see the bearded hijacker sitting inside. He had a long nose and dark hair and his eyes looked green from the light of the instruments in the dark cabin. He held his gun near his mouth and touched it gently with his lips as he waited.

Carl had heard half of the conversation. Eight of the ten minutes had gone. Now that he could do nothing, he felt afraid. He could feel his hand in the handcuffs shaking. Harald felt it too and held Carl's hand with his own.

'Don't worry, Mr Sandberg,' Harald whispered. 'We'll get out of here.'

'Perhaps,' Carl answered. 'And perhaps not. But I don't want these murderers to go free.'

'Ssh!' Harald whispered. Carl looked up and saw the girl watching them. Then, suddenly, the bearded man shouted, 'They're coming! Look! Get ready!'

The girl went into the Captain's cabin. Harald and Carl stood up and looked through a window. They saw three men pushing some steps across the tarmac. The men put the steps outside the plane door and then went back again. Then two more men came out of the building. They were wearing bright yellow coats because of the rain. One man walked towards the plane.

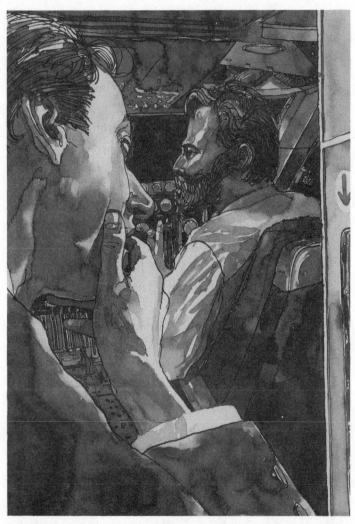

Carl could see the bearded hijacker from the light of the instruments.

'Come away from the door! Quick!' The girl unlocked the handcuffs and pushed Harald and Carl back to their seats. Then she started to open the door.

'Wait! Turn the lights out and stand back from the door!' said the bearded man. 'They will try to shoot us in the light from the door.'

The door opened and the man in the yellow coat came into the plane. He was thin, with very short hair. The girl shut the door, the lights came on, and the man shut his eyes in the bright light. The girl and the bearded man put their arms around him, laughing.

'Free! You are free now, brother! And the other one, is he safe? Come into the cabin, let's talk!'

Carl and Harald watched sadly. 'So now she will give them what they want, because of me,' said Carl quietly. 'We will be safe, but they will go free to bomb another plane, because of me.' He held his head in his hands.

'Wait, Mr Sandberg,' said Harald. 'Your wife isn't stupid, you know. This game has not ended yet. Sit still, and be ready.'

The other passengers sat quietly, waiting to be free.

13

Helen Sandberg stood by the control room window, staring at the plane. 'Come on,' she said. 'Why is that door shut? Where are the passengers?'

'Free! You are free now, brother!'

'The hijackers won't set them free,' said Inspector Holm. 'I told you, Prime Minister, this is a serious mistake.'

'Be quiet, man,' said Colonel Carter. 'I think we've got something on the radio.'

Beside him, a soldier was turning the controls of a small army radio. Suddenly, the voices of one of the hijackers and the prisoner came into the room.

'So how many soldiers are there in the airport building, my brother?'

'I didn't see any soldiers, only police.'

'That's strange! No soldiers at all?'

'I did not see any, brother.'

'Very strange. But these are not military people. They do not have many soldiers. Perhaps the woman will do what she says, then.'

'What's happening, Colonel?' Helen asked. 'Those are the hijackers' voices. How can we hear them?'

The Colonel laughed. 'Well, madam, you can see it's raining, can't you? We didn't want our poor prisoner to get wet, so we gave him a nice yellow raincoat, you see. But it was an expensive raincoat, because one of its buttons is a small radio transmitter. So now we can hear everything they say and we know where they are on the plane!'

Helen smiled. 'Good idea, Colonel. I hope it helps.'

'Prime Minister,' Michael interrupted. 'They're coming!'

Helen looked through the window. The door of the

47

plane was open and people were coming down the steps one after another. Some of them started to run towards the airport building, and a few knelt down on the wet tarmac.

'What are they doing?' Helen asked.

'Praying, perhaps?' said Michael. 'To thank God that they're alive?'

Police and doctors came out of the building to help the passengers. Helen stood and watched through the binoculars. She did not see Carl.

'Ninety-nine, a hundred. That's it, then,' said Colonel Carter. The plane door closed. 'Now we move on to the next step of our plan. Goodbye, Prime Minister.'

Helen turned and saw that the Colonel was putting on white clothes on top of his army uniform. He put several grenades in the coat pocket, and a machine gun into a long pocket inside the coat. He smiled at her. 'I must help my men refuel the plane.'

'May God go with you, Colonel,' she said.

14

The lights in the plane went out again. There were only eleven of them left now: Carl Sandberg and Harald, four crew, and five Americans. They sat together in the middle of the plane. The girl and the young man in the black shirt watched them.

The Colonel put some grenades in the coat pocket.

Through the window, Carl saw the fuel tanker drive towards the plane. It stopped, and five men in white clothes got out. The pilot went to the front of the plane to work the controls, and the men started to refuel the plane.

Then he saw another man in a yellow raincoat come out of the airport building.

The bearded hijacker started to talk very excitedly. 'Is it him? Yes, it is! Our leader! My brother and sister, we have done it! Now, I must welcome him at the door. You, brother, watch the pilot in the cabin, and sister, watch the passengers.'

Carl Sandberg watched the man in the yellow coat walk nearer. He could only see one man at the back of the plane, refuelling it. He thought the others were under the plane somewhere, but he did not know where.

Harald put his hand on Carl's arm. Carl looked at him. Harald did not speak, but he was looking at the girl, very carefully.

As the door opened, and the man with the yellow coat came in, the girl turned to look. Through the window, Carl saw a man in a white coat run out from under the plane with something that looked like a grenade in his hand. Two other men in white ran out behind him.

The man's arm went up and he threw the grenade through the open door. There was a very loud *BANG!* at the front of the plane, and a flash of white light that burned Carl's eyes. Almost immediately there was an even louder *BANG! BANG!* and two more flashes of white light.

Carl could not move. The noise was so loud and the light so bright that he sat still as a stone. He saw the girl hijacker and the bearded man standing quite still too, with their guns in their hands and their mouths open. Then a man in white ran through the door with a gun in his hand. He shot the girl and the bearded man before they could move. The hijacker in the black shirt came out of the Captain's cabin behind the man in white, but two other men in white came through the door and shot him too. The two prisoners, in their yellow raincoats, tried to get to the door, but the men in white knocked them to the floor and handcuffed their hands behind their backs.

Carl looked down. The girl was lying on the floor of the aisle beside him. He thought he saw her hand move towards her machine gun, but then one of the soldiers in white ran down the aisle and shot her again through the head. Another soldier pulled her away by her legs and her long hair left blood along the floor.

15

Helen Sandberg heard the bangs too, and when she saw the white light, she thought the plane was burning. For about half a minute there was nothing but loud bangs and white flashes, and then there was nothing. There were no lights at all in the plane and no sounds either.

She turned to Michael. 'Can't you get them on the radio?'

'I'm trying, Prime Minister. But I think it's broken.'

She walked to the door. 'I'm going out.'

Inspector Holm stood in front of her. 'You must not do that, Prime Minister. We don't know what's happened.'

'That's why I'm going,' she said. 'I'm going to find out. I don't care what happens to me.'

He was a big man but he was afraid of her. She walked straight past him and down the steps. In the departure lounge there was a crowd of passengers waiting to get on other planes, and also a lot of doctors, police, and newspaper journalists. She walked straight past them all and out onto the tarmac. It was dark and cold, and the wind blew rain into her face. When she was about fifty metres away from the building she heard some people behind her, but she did not stop.

The door of the plane opened and a man in white came out. He had a gun in his hand and he came backwards down the steps. After him came two men in yellow raincoats with their hands behind their backs, and then two other men in white with guns.

Two police officers came after her.

'Wait, Prime Minister,' they said. 'Please stop, it's dangerous.'

'I'm going to find out. I don't care what happens to me.'

'Not now,' she said. 'It's not dangerous any more.' She walked on through the rain without stopping, and the young police officers walked beside her. They were afraid to touch her and they did not know what to do. Some journalists ran after them.

Two men in blue came out of the plane – the pilot and co-pilot. Then some men in suits. She was quite near the plane now and there were quite a lot of newspaper photographers around her, but she did not stop walking.

A big young man came out of the plane with a short, thin, grey-haired one – Harald and Carl. Helen could see that Carl's face was very white and there was blood on his mouth, but he could walk all right.

Carl saw her coming, a small strong figure walking through the rain, with a crowd of police and photographers around her. 'Harald, my friend,' he said. 'I think we're in the news again. You're going to have another photo to show your little son on his birthday.'

Carl and Helen Sandberg met at the bottom of the steps in the darkness and the rain. And Carl was right; there was a photo of it in every newspaper in the world the next day.

GLOSSARY

aboard   on a plane or a ship

advise   to tell someone what they should do

aisle   a place between lines of seats (e.g. on a plane, in a theatre) where you can walk

ambassador   a person sent to a foreign country to speak for his own country's government

attack *(v)*   to try to hurt someone or something

bend (past tense **bent**)   to turn the top half of the body downwards

binoculars   very strong glasses used to see things far away

cabin   a room on a plane or a ship

chest   the front part of the body between the neck and stomach

colonel   an important officer in the army

commando section   a group of soldiers specially trained for making quick attacks

control room   the building in an airport where people control air traffic by radio

crew   the pilot and all the people who work on a plane

deal with   to do something that needs doing

decision   what you have decided

departure lounge   a room in an airport where passengers wait

embassy   the building where an ambassador lives and works

fire *(v)*   to shoot a gun

fist   a closed hand with fingers turned inwards

flash *(n)*   a sudden, very bright light for a very short time

flight   a journey on a plane

forehead   the part of the face above the eyes

freedom   being free; able to do what you want to do

fuel tanker   a large vehicle for carrying petrol

gentleman   a polite word for a man

goddam *(adj, slang)*   a word used to show you feel strongly
  about something (e.g. goddam plane)

government   the group of people who control a country

groan *(v)*   to make a deep, sad sound

handcuff *(v)*   to lock someone's hands together with handcuffs
  (metal rings around the wrists)

hell   a word used with question-words (e.g. Where the hell . . .)
  to show anger or surprise

hijacker   a person who takes control of a plane and makes the
  pilot fly to a different place

homework   schoolwork which you do at home

honey   a word for someone you love very much

hostess   a woman who takes care of passengers on a plane

innocent   an 'innocent' person has done nothing bad or wrong

inspector   an important police officer

instruments   in a plane, instruments tell the pilot how high the
  plane is, how much fuel there is, etc.

interrupt   to stop somebody talking by speaking yourself

journalist   a person who writes for newspapers, television, etc.

kneel (past tense **knelt**)   to go down or stay with your knees on
  the ground

liberation   freedom

list *(n)*   a piece of paper with names written on it

local time   the time in the place you are talking about

ma'am   madam; a polite way of speaking to a woman

machine gun   a gun that fires a lot of bullets very fast

marine   a soldier who is trained to fight on land or sea

military base   a place where soldiers live and work

military men   men from an army; soldiers

nervous afraid

on time neither late nor early; at the agreed or correct time

open-necked with the top buttons of a shirt undone

pause *(v)* to stop for a moment; **pause** *(n)* a short stop

pig a farm animal; in this story, a word for a very bad person

point *(v)* to show with your hand or finger where something is

pool some liquid (water, blood, etc.) on the ground

pour to put liquids (water, tea, coffee, etc.) into something

power people like prime ministers, presidents, etc. have power; they can tell other people what to do

pray to talk to God

press *(v)* to push hard

prime minister the most important person in a government

refuel to bring more fuel to a plane, ship, etc.

SAS Special Air Service; specially trained British soldiers who are used for difficult kinds of fighting, e.g. against terrorists

set free to make someone free, e.g. from a prison, from a hijack

skyjack a hijack in the air

sweat water that comes out of the skin when you are hot or afraid

take apart to destroy; to win a battle in a very violent way

tarmac a hard material used for roads, airports, etc.

tear *(n)* water that comes from your eyes when you cry

tear (past tense **tore**) to pull something to pieces

terrorists very violent people who kill, or promise to kill, other people if they don't get what they want

throw (past tense **threw**) to make something move through the air

tough (of a person) strong, hard, brave

transmitter a radio that sends messages

tray a piece of wood (or plastic, etc.) for carrying food and drink

Skyjack!

ACTIVITIES

Before Reading

1 Read the story introduction on the first page of the book, and the back cover. How much do you know now about the story? Choose **Y** (Yes) or **N** (No) for each sentence.

   1 People who hijack a plane are terrorists. Y/N
   2 The hijackers are using bombs to kill the passengers. Y/N
   3 The Prime Minister is on the plane. Y/N
   4 Someone from the Prime Minister's family is on the plane. Y/N
   5 The hijackers know who this person is. Y/N
   6 The hijackers will wait for hours if they have to. Y/N

2 **What should you do if you are a passenger on a hijacked plane? Look at these ideas and decide which are sensible and which are not sensible. Explain why you think this.**

   If your plane is hijacked you should . . .
   1 . . . stay in your seat and be very quiet.
   2 . . . argue with the hijackers and tell them they are stupid.
   3 . . . tell jokes and try to make the hijackers laugh.
   4 . . . talk loudly to show you are not afraid.
   5 . . . try to remember what the hijackers look like.
   6 . . . draw a picture of the hijackers to show to the police.
   7 . . . try to attack the hijackers and get their guns.
   8 . . . pretend to feel very ill and ask for a doctor.

While Reading

Read Chapters 1 to 7. Choose the best question-word for these questions, and then answer them.

Who / What / How / Why

Carl's story – Chapters 1, 2, 4, 6

1 . . . was Harald's job?
2 . . . was the air hostess holding when she came out of the pilot's cabin?
3 . . . many hijackers were there?
4 . . . group did the hijackers belong to?
5 . . . long were the two prisoners in prison for?
6 . . . did Harald put coffee on Carl's passport and eat it?
7 . . . did Harald say to the hijacker about Carl?
8 . . . did the hijackers take to the front of the plane?
9 . . . do you think Carl is?

Helen's story – Chapters 3, 5, 7

1 . . . did Helen Sandberg groan at 12.15 a.m.?
2 . . . many people were there on the plane?
3 . . . three things did the hijackers want?
4 . . . did the hijackers say they would do in one hour's time?
5 . . . did the short fat man die?
6 . . . did Colonel Carter want to do?
7 . . . was Helen angry with Inspector Holm?
8 . . . arrived at the airport to see Helen?

**Read Chapters 8 to 11. Are these sentences true (T) or false (F)?
Rewrite the false ones with the correct information.**

Carl's story – Chapters 8, 10

1 The girl fired her gun in the plane because an American
   passenger hit her.
2 Harald knocked two of the terrorists to the ground.
3 Nobody tried to help Harald when he attacked.
4 The hijackers handcuffed Harald to the door.
5 The hijackers learnt who Carl was from the newspaper
   photograph in Harald's pocket.
6 Carl argued with the girl because he was afraid.
7 Carl told her that the man who died was a spy.
8 When the girl was young, her family were very poor.
9 Carl felt sorry for the girl and Harald.

Helen's story – Chapters 9, 11

1 Helen liked both the ambassadors.
2 Both ambassadors wanted to use their own soldiers to
   attack the plane.
3 Helen thought it was a good idea to attack the plane and
   'take it apart'.
4 The hijackers knew that Carl was the Prime Minister's
   husband.
5 Helen and the Colonel made a plan together.
6 Helen told the hijackers that she needed another twenty
   minutes to get the prisoners.
7 The hijackers said they would wait for ten minutes.
8 The hijackers wanted Carl and Harald to go with them to
   another country.

Before you read Chapters 12 to 15, can you guess the answers to these questions?

1 Will Inspector Holm arrive with the prisoners in time?
2 Will Colonel Carter take the plane from the hijackers?
3 Will Carl or Harald be hurt in the attack?
4 Will any of the other passengers or crew be killed?
5 Will the three hijackers be killed or put in prison?
6 Will the two prisoners be killed or taken back to prison?

Read Chapters 12 to 15. Then put these sentences in the right order, to make a summary.

1 He and his men drove the fuel tanker to the plane, and began to refuel it.
2 A few minutes later one hundred passengers left the plane.
3 The two prisoners were knocked down and handcuffed.
4 She met her husband at the bottom of the plane steps.
5 The two prisoners, both wearing yellow raincoats, came out of the airport building.
6 As he entered the plane, one of the soldiers threw a grenade through the open door.
7 The first prisoner crossed the tarmac and went into the plane.
8 More grenades exploded, and then the soldiers ran in and shot the three hijackers.
9 When the plane door closed again, the Colonel got ready.
10 Then the second prisoner crossed the tarmac to the plane.
11 When the noise of grenades and guns stopped, Helen began to walk across the tarmac to the plane.

63

After Reading

1 **What did Colonel Carter tell Helen about his plan? Put their conversation in the right order, and write in the speakers' names. Helen speaks first (number 5).**

1 _____ 'That's the plan, Prime Minister. We'll wear white coats, like mechanics, and drive the fuel tanker up to the plane.'

2 _____ 'Right. And when he's on the plane, they must let one hundred passengers out, as they agreed.'

3 _____ 'When they open the door for the second prisoner, we'll throw in grenades, and attack at once.'

4 _____ 'They'll be all right. For a few seconds, during the grenade attack, the hijackers won't be able to move. A few seconds is all we need.'

5 _____ 'We haven't got much time, Colonel. What are we going to do?'

6 _____ 'Ah, the refuelling. So you and your men—?'

7 _____ 'The most important thing for the terrorists is the prisoners. So when they arrive, we'll send one to the plane at once.'

8 _____ 'But what about the passengers still inside?'

9 _____ 'Yes. We wait until those hundred passengers are on the tarmac. Then we must refuel the plane.'

10 _____ 'Well, good luck, Colonel.'

11 _____ 'Excellent! And how will you get inside the plane?'

2 Perhaps one of the passengers who was on the plane at the end wrote to a friend about the hijack. Complete the letter with these words from the story. (Use one word in each gap.)

aisle, ambassador, attack, bang, before, bullets, commandos, die, fired, flash, fuel, grenades, handcuffed, hijack, hijackers, machine, nervous, seconds, ship, shot, shouted, tarmac, worst

Dear Sam

I'm staying in the US _____'s house here, with the other four Americans that were in the _____ with me. I'm fine, but all of us still get very _____ when we hear a sudden _____ or there's a _____ of bright light. It'll take time, I suppose.

It was a terrible thing, Sam. I think the _____ moment was when they _____ poor Bill. It was the girl who did it, too. I stood up and _____ at her, and she _____ her _____ gun at me. I felt the _____ going through my hair.

There was one brave man who ran up the _____ and tried to _____ the _____. He didn't win, of course. They _____ him to the door and told him he'd be the next to _____.

When I saw the _____ tanker coming, I knew what was going to happen. Those _____ were good, Sam. They came straight in after the _____ and got the hijackers _____ they could move. It was all over in _____.

But when we got out of the plane, there was poor Bill's body, just lying on the _____. I'll never forget that.

I'll see you in a few weeks – I'm coming home by _____!
Best wishes,

Jim

3 **Perhaps this is what some of the characters in the story were thinking. Which five characters were they, and what was happening in the story at that moment?**

  1 Poor Prime Minister! She looks so worried. Now that the hijackers know that Carl is her husband, it's even worse for her. Giving her that message was the most unpleasant thing I've ever had to do . . .

  2 Maybe this is my chance to do something . . . That girl is very young and nervous, and she's crying. She's probably never fired a gun and killed someone before. Nobody's looking at us at the moment. If I run quickly, perhaps I can get one of the guns . . .

  3 That stupid woman has no idea how to deal with terrorists. They really need a man to make these decisions. Well, I've got the prisoners, and I'm not in a hurry. If anyone asks, I'll say . . . there's been an accident.

  4 I hope she's going to listen to me this time. She's an intelligent woman, but she's quite difficult sometimes. I'm sure our SAS men could deal with this – better than her own soldiers. Ah, they're calling us in to see her now . . .

  5 I feel so nervous. It's easy for the others – they just have to sit and be passengers. I'm the one who has to talk to people and do things. They must do it soon, surely. Or we'll – yes! He's waving to me! At last! Now the PLA can begin its work, and soon our brothers will be free. . .

4 Here are some titles for the fifteen chapters of *Skyjack*. Write the number of each chapter next to its title and write them out in the correct order.

_____ The girl's story
_____ Blood on the tarmac
_____ Welcome aboard
_____ A change of plan
_____ Helen, Carl and Harald
_____ The PLA choose a passenger
_____ One brother in a yellow coat
_____ Helen agrees with the hijackers
_____ The Colonel, the Inspector, and the Prime Minister
_____ Meeting the ambassadors
_____ Mummy is late
_____ The passengers leave
_____ Bang, flash – death
_____ Harald is brave
_____ Coffee and – a passport

5 What do you think about hijacking? Do you agree (A) or disagree (D) with these sentences? Explain why.

1 Helen was wrong to bring the prisoners to the airport.
2 The girl hijacker had good reasons to be a terrorist.
3 The soldiers were wrong to kill the hijackers.
4 Harald was stupid to try and take the hijackers' guns.
5 It is always wrong to give hijackers what they want.
6 If you are fighting to win your freedom, sometimes it is necessary to do things like hijacking.

ABOUT THE AUTHOR

Tim Vicary is an experienced teacher and writer, and has written several stories for the Oxford Bookworms Library. Many of these are in the Thriller & Adventure series, such as *Chemical Secret* (at Stage 3), or in the True Stories series, such as *The Brontë Story* (also at Stage 3), which is about the lives of the famous novelists, Charlotte, Emily, and Anne Brontë.

Tim Vicary has two children, and keeps dogs, cats, and horses. He lives and works in York, in the north of England, and has also published two long novels, *The Blood upon the Rose* and *Cat and Mouse*.

ABOUT BOOKWORMS

OXFORD BOOKWORMS LIBRARY
Classics • True Stories • Fantasy & Horror • Human Interest
Crime & Mystery • Thriller & Adventure

The OXFORD BOOKWORMS LIBRARY offers a wide range of original and adapted stories, both classic and modern, which take learners from elementary to advanced level through six carefully graded language stages:

Stage 1 (400 headwords)	**Stage 4** (1400 headwords)
Stage 2 (700 headwords)	**Stage 5** (1800 headwords)
Stage 3 (1000 headwords)	**Stage 6** (2500 headwords)

More than fifty titles are also available on cassette, and there are many titles at Stages 1 to 4 which are specially recommended for younger learners. In addition to the introductions and activities in each Bookworm, resource material includes photocopiable test worksheets and Teacher's Handbooks, which contain advice on running a class library and using cassettes, and the answers for the activities in the books.

Several other series are linked to the OXFORD BOOKWORMS LIBRARY. They range from highly illustrated readers for young learners, to playscripts, non-fiction readers, and unsimplified texts for advanced learners.

Oxford Bookworms Starters　　　　*Oxford Bookworms Factfiles*
Oxford Bookworms Playscripts　　　*Oxford Bookworms Collection*

Details of these series and a full list of all titles in the OXFORD BOOKWORMS LIBRARY can be found in the *Oxford English* catalogues. A selection of titles from the OXFORD BOOKWORMS LIBRARY can be found on the next pages.

Wyatt's Hurricane

DESMOND BAGLEY

Retold by Jennifer Bassett

Hurricane Mabel is far out in the Atlantic Ocean and moving slowly northwards. Perhaps it will never come near land at all. But if it hits the island of San Fernandez, many thousands of people will die. There could be winds of more than 250 kilometres an hour. There could be a huge tidal wave from the sea, which will drown the capital city of St Pierre. Mabel will destroy houses, farms, roads, bridges . . .

Only one man, David Wyatt, believes that Mabel will hit San Fernandez, but nobody will listen to him . . .

Chemical Secret

TIM VICARY

The job was too good. There had to be a problem – and there was.

John Duncan was an honest man, but he needed money. He had children to look after. He was ready to do anything, and his bosses knew it.

They gave him the job because he couldn't say no; he couldn't afford to be honest. And the job was like a poison inside him. It changed him and blinded him, so that he couldn't see the real poison – until it was too late.

On the Edge

GILLIAN CROSS

Retold by Clare West

When Tug wakes up, he is not in his own bedroom at home. The
door is locked and there are bars across the window. Loud music
hammers through the house and through his head. Then a woman
comes in and says that she is his mother, but Tug knows that she
is *not* his mother . . .

Outside, Jinny stares through the trees at the lonely house on
the hill. She hears strange noises, but she turns away. After all, it's
none of her business . . .

The Crown of Violet

GEOFFREY TREASE

Retold by John Escott

High up on a stone seat in the great open-air theatre of Athens,
Alexis, son of Leon, watches the Festival of Plays – and dreams of
seeing his own play on that famous stage.

So, as the summer passes, Alexis writes his play for the next
year's Festival. But then, with his friend Corinna, he learns that
Athens has enemies – enemies who do not like Athenian
democracy, and who are planning a revolution to end it all . . .

Justice

TIM VICARY

London: November.

Terrorists blow up the Queen's coach outside Parliament. The Queen escapes, but five people are killed, and forty others badly hurt – ordinary, innocent people, like Alan Cole, the Queen's coachman, who loses his leg in the bombing. And for Alan and his daughter Jane there is more terror to come, in the search for the truth behind the bombing. Will the terrorists be caught and brought to justice?

But what kind of justice? What can give Alan Cole his leg back, or give life back to people who have been blown to pieces by a bomb?

Reflex

DICK FRANCIS

Retold by Rowena Akinyemi

People who ride racehorses love the speed, the excitement, the danger – and winning the race. Philip Nore has been riding for many years and he always wants to win – but sometimes he is told to lose. Why?

And what is the mystery about the photographer, George Millace, who has just died in a car crash?

Philip Nore knows the answer to the first question, and he wants to find out the answer to the second. But as he begins to learn George Millace's secrets, he realizes that his own life is in danger.